BRAD'S BRAINWAVE

BY JILL MCDOUGALL

ILLUSTRATED BY DANI JONES

Pearson Australia
(a division of Pearson Australia Group Pty Ltd)
707 Collins Street, Melbourne, Victoria 3008
PO Box 23360, Melbourne, Victoria 8012
www.pearson.com.au

First published 2012 by Pearson Australia
2015 2014 2013 2012
10 9 8 7 6 5 4 3 2 1

Commissioning Editor: Sabine Bolick
Project Editor: Suzy Freeman
Editor: Sophie Ayerbe
Designer: Glen McClay
Copyright & Pictures Editor: Marg Barber
Illustrator: Dani Jones
Printed in Australia by the SOS Print + Media Group

ISBN 978 1 4425 3779 8
Pearson Australia Group Pty Ltd ABN 40 004 245 943

★CONTENTS★

CHAPTER 1

SUNDAY

"IT'S A DISASTER," says Rusty.

"It's more than a disaster—it's a world-class catastrophe."

Rusty and I are staring at the sign on the pizza shop window. It's just before five o'clock on Sunday afternoon. The pizza shop never opens until five. That isn't the problem. It's the rest of the sign that makes my eyeballs wobble.

Rusty makes a face like a bulldog. "The Angelos' pizzas are the best in Westville," he groans.

"They're the *only* pizzas in Westville," I moan.

Rusty nods as if he's just invented nodding. "Exactly my point, Einstein. What now?"

Rusty is my best friend and fellow member of the local Under-12 soccer team, the Westville Warriors. His face is covered in freckles, and his red hair is gelled into spiky tufts. If someone wrote a profile of Rusty, it would look a bit like this:

★RUSSELL NAILSWORTH★

Nickname: Rusty (as in Rusty Nail)

Age: 10 ¾

Favourite sport: Soccer

Favourite position: Winger

Claim to fame: Top scorer last season

Me? I'm Brad, but my friends call me Einstein after the brainy scientist. Some say it's because my last name is Skully (*Skull-y*, get it?). Here's the full picture:

★BRAD SKULLY★

Nickname: Einstein

Age: 11 ½

Favourite sport: Soccer

Favourite position: Striker

Claim to fame: Captain of the Westville Warriors

I reckon the real reason people call me Einstein is because of my super-brilliant ***brainwaves***. I'm having one right now. A scary one.

I stare through the window of the pizza shop at the piles of untidy boxes on the floor. "You don't think the Angelos are leaving town, do you?" I ask Rusty.

His eyebrows shoot up. "The Angelos? No way."

I rap on the door until Nick Angelo opens up. He must be helping his dad. Nick is pretty short for an eleven-year-old but he's built for speed. He's the star player of our team, and I do mean star.

★NICK ANGELO★

Nickname: Nicko

Age: 12

Favourite sport: Soccer

Favourite position: All

Claim to fame: Best at everything

Get the idea? Without Nick, the Westville Warriors would have another season licking the wooden spoon. Instead, this Saturday we're playing in the grand final. ***Un-bee-lievable!***

Nick wears a pained expression. I don't think it's from the hot salami on the pizza he's munching. "Hi guys," he says, wiping dribble from his chin. "Guess what! I'm off."

"Off? What do you mean 'off'?"

"Leaving town. Heading south."

I give a fake-cheerful laugh. This is worse than I expected. "Er … when will that be?"

Nick sucks in more pizza. He's a human vacuum cleaner. "Tomorrow."

"Tomorrow? As in the day after today?"

"Uh huh. We just found out."

"You're ***bailing*** out before the grand final?" Rusty chimes in, looking fierce.

"Yeah, sorry about that," says Nick. He doesn't look sorry. In fact, his pizza-chomping mouth breaks into a grin. "I'm trying out for the Wildcats in the city." He pauses for effect. "Next Saturday."

Rusty and I wander back down the street

in a state of shock. On the way we pass:

The Westville Laundromat (closed down).

The Westville DVD shop (closed down).

The Westville Hairdressing Salon (closed down).

The Westville Primary School (closed down—but only for the holidays).

It's like walking through a ghost town. A ghost town in a desert. Westville used to be all green and leafy, edged by a wide, flowing river. Now it's dusty and brown alongside a string of dirty puddles.

The problem, in case you haven't guessed, is ***rain***. There hasn't been any for as long as I can remember, and the town is dying.

This week though, Westville is putting on a happy face. Fences and shops are decked out in blue and gold balloons and streamers (the Warrior colours). People greet Rusty and me like we're superheroes.

"Go the mighty ***Warr-iors!***" calls Mrs Gutenberg from the bakery.

"You boys rock!" pipes up Shirley from Westville Fruit and Veg.

"Warriors to win!" booms Mr Wright as we pass the tiny newspaper office. He jabs his finger at the front page of the *Westville Weekly* taped to the window.

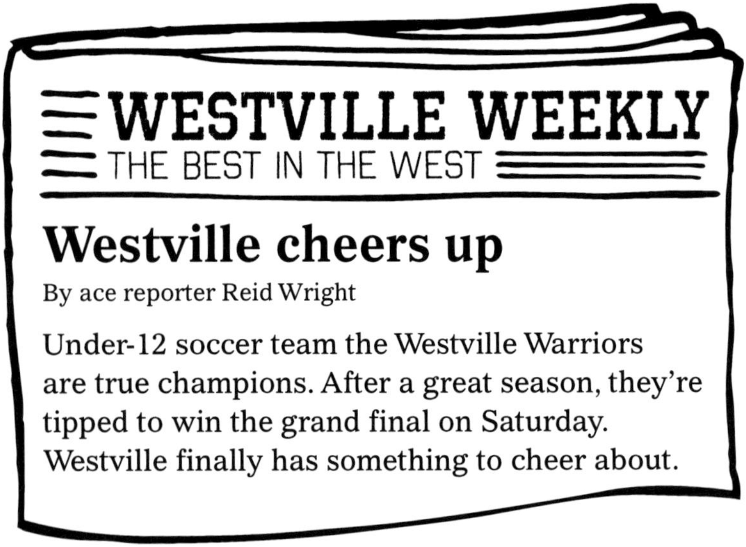

WESTVILLE WEEKLY

THE BEST IN THE WEST

Westville cheers up

By ace reporter Reid Wright

Under-12 soccer team the Westville Warriors are true champions. After a great season, they're tipped to win the grand final on Saturday. Westville finally has something to cheer about.

We cross the road towards the sports ground. Rusty flips off his cap and spikes up his hair. Then he puts his cap back on. His face is serious. “The only thing keeping this town going is the grand final,” he says.

I plonk onto the grass. That’s right, grass! The sports ground is the only green spot in town, thanks to the locals who keep it going with buckets of grey water from washing machines and showers.

“There won’t be a grand final unless we can fill Nick’s spot,” I say glumly. “We’re down to eight players. That’s one less than we can legally play with.”

I lean on my elbows and watch a team of ants carting a monstrous beetle across a bald patch. They'll never make it.

"Trouble is, every guy our age is already on the team," Rusty says. He picks a scab off his knee and flicks it the air. It lands on the leader of the ant team.

I stare at Rusty. Not because of the scab flicking but because I feel a sudden attack of genius coming on.

"Every guy is on the team except one," I say slowly. I swing my arm in a circle as if I'm bowling a cricket ball.

Rusty's eyes stab into mine. "You don't mean—?"

"Yep. Zola the Bowler."

Rusty jumps to his feet and runs across the soccer pitch squawking and flapping his arms.

"AAAAAAA," he screeches. ***"AAAAAAAAAAAAA!"*** He stops. "Imagine the glory! Zola the Bowler—a Westville Warrior!"

I beam at him. "Pretty cool, huh?"

"Dead right. Are you going to ask him straight out?"

"Maybe."

He shakes his head. "He'll never agree."

"He has to," I say, getting to my feet. "He's our only hope."

CHAPTER 2

MONDAY: FIVE DAYS TO GO

IF SOMEONE WROTE A PROFILE of Zola the Bowler, it would look like this:

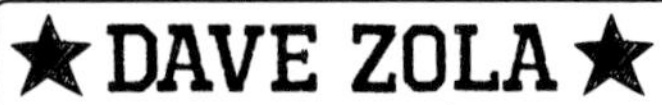

Nickname: Zola the Bowler (or just Zola)
Age: Nearly 12
Favourite sport: Cricket
Favourite position: Bowler
Claim to fame: Plays in the state schoolboys' team

I chew this over as I pedal my old BMX (two sizes too small) along the gravel road to 'Upson Downs', the Zolas' farm. Stones clack under my wheels. Seed pods snap and crackle like breakfast cereal. My armpits are steamy enough to defrost Antarctica.

The Zolas' house is on top of a rise, looking over empty, brown paddocks. I'm nearly there when a quad bike roars towards me with a massive **vrrommmp**. Dave Zola spins the wheels like he's in the Quad Bike Olympics. With a gut-churning loop, he skids to a halt just in front of me. The engine stutters into silence.

Zola's legs are about three storeys high, and he moves like one of those water birds you see around dams—graceful, you'd call it. His eyes are friendly but wary.

I'm about to blurt out something dumb when I have one of my famous brainwaves. "How about a hit?" I ask, nodding towards the custom-made gravel cricket pitch in his front yard.

His eyes switch to high beam. "Sure thing."

I grab the bat and turn my elbow down the pitch. I've played a bit of cricket, but I'm not in Zola's league. His big left hand hangs loosely around the ball. He takes a run up, straightens his arm and a red missile whizzes past my wrist.

Clunk! I'm out.

The next ball crunches into my knee.

The next bounces off the grass and scatters the wickets like chopsticks.

Crack! Zam! Pow!

Zola is a super-charged bowling machine.

When the massacre is over, we settle into wicker chairs on the front verandah with a cool drink.

It's peaceful here. Sheep baa. Magpies chortle. Insects buzz. Zola spins a cricket ball in his fingers and slurps water.

"What d'you think about soccer?" I blurt.

The ball stops spinning. "I don't."

"Don't what?"

"Think about soccer."

"Oh," I gulp.

This isn't going well. I try again. "Well anyway...d'you want to play for the Warriors?"

He frowns as though I've just offered him a plate of slugs. "Why would I?"

I give him the lowdown on the team's (desperate) situation. His head shakes and nods, and shakes again as he listens.

"I'll give it a go," he says at last.

Excellent!

He tosses me the ball. "But only if you can bowl me out."

Oh.

We saunter over to the cricket pitch. I pretend to tie up my shoelaces, stalling for time. Zola takes up a spot at the wicket and looks pleased with himself. He's too polite to give me a straight-out "no". This way, it's all up to me, and Zola is pretty sure I can't bowl for peanuts.

I have a surprise for him. I'm pretty useless with the bat but when it comes to bowling, I know a few sneaky tricks. I take a run up, flick my wrist and—***wham!***

The ball goes wide.

I try again, and this time the ball nicks the inside edge of his bat. I'm getting closer to the big one.

I spit on the ball and polish it on the front of my shorts. Then I hide the ball deep in the palm of my hand. I pretend I'm about to bowl a ripper, but the ball leaves my hand like a dead weight and glides through the air at snail speed.

Zola takes a swipe, but at the last moment, the ball swings in.

Crack! The bails fly.

Zola's mouth gapes open like a stunned fish.

"Soccer training is on tomorrow arvo. Four o'clock at the sports ground," I tell him as I collect my bike helmet.

I jump on my bike. Then, I turn and spin the wheels hard as I blast down the driveway.

Mission accomplished.

CHAPTER 3

TUESDAY: FOUR DAYS TO GO

OUR HOUSE IS OPPOSITE the sports ground and it stands out like a sore thumb.

Clue: Look for piles of rusty springs and metal pipes in the front yard. You might think it's a bunch of rubbish but take a closer look. You'll see that each pile is welded together to make little animals.

Dad started making animals out of junk after the rainwater tank business went bust. No-one around here can afford a new rainwater tank. Not until the drought breaks.

No-one can afford metal pigs either, but it gives Dad something to do.

I stand on the back verandah munching an apple. A hissing noise comes from the big open shed and blue sparks fly. Dad's welding a new project. It's a heavy-duty sculpture made from barbed wire and bathtubs. He flips up his helmet and flashes me a grin. "I'm calling this one 'Wired'."

If you ask me, ***Weird*** would suit it better.

My little brother Simon is on his knees in the vegie patch peering inside a cauliflower. He's a total maths freak, and right now he's into fractals. Does that sound like something out of a spaceship? Fractals are made up of shapes inside shapes, inside shapes. They're in clouds and leaves and yep…cauliflowers. Simon treats the whole world like one giant maths puzzle.

I'm about to head off to soccer practice when the phone rings. We don't use the mobile anymore. Mum reckons it costs too much.

"It's for you, Brad."

The voice at the other end sounds like a walrus honking. It takes a while to recognise Jake, our soccer coach.

"What's up, bro?"

Jake's in Year 12 and he's into hip-hop, so I try to talk at his level.

More honks and a couple of snorts rattle down the phone line.

"You got the flu, dude?"

It turns out Jake has more than the flu. He's in hospital with full-on pneumonia. He says he'll be better in a couple of weeks. In the meantime …

I whistle through my teeth. The Westville Warriors are flying solo all the way to that sweet silver trophy. As captain, it's up to me to make it happen.

No sweat. We've got Zola the Bowler. We can't lose!

"The aim is to get the ball into the net," I explain patiently.

Zola nods. Someone forgot to tell him that soccer players wear shorts. He's dressed in cricket whites.

Soccer practice is not going well. On a scale of one to ten, I'd give it minus seventeen. Zola is a cricket star but he doesn't know a thing about soccer. To cover up, he acts like we don't know anything either. The boys gather round, offering advice.

"The soccer goal is like the wickets," says Rusty. "Aim for the net."

"Got it," mumbles Zola. But he looks confused.

"And don't rub the ball on your pants."

"Are you sure?"

"Yes!"

"Okay. I'll kick it dirty then."

"Don't kick the ball with your toes, Zola."

"Why not?"

"You'll hurt yourself."

"Really?"

"Yeah! Kick it with the top of your boot."

"Are you sure?"

"YES!" we all yell.

Zola takes a dozen steps back and charges the ball with his arms swinging as if he's about to bowl a spinner down the crease.

"No!" we all yell.

Did I say minus seventeen? Make that minus 117!

By the time soccer practice is over, one thing is clear. With Zola on our team, we wouldn't beat a bunch of Year Ones.

Luckily, Zola gets the message. "Guess I'll stick with cricket," he says, looking down.

The team gathers round with dismal faces. "Great brainwave, Einstein."

Not.

"If we don't have nine players on Saturday, we'll have to forfeit," says Rusty, chewing hard on his lip.

Forfeit. I hate that word. My spirits sink straight to my boots, setting a new world record for speed.

It's time to go to brainwave number two.

If only I had one.

CHAPTER 4

WEDNESDAY: THREE DAYS TO GO

"**GIVE ME A HAND** in the kitchen, love. You've been moping around the house all morning."

Moping. So that's what you call it. I thought it was a bad case of ***Major Freak-out*** mixed with ***Mega-normous Panic***. The grand final is three days away and we still don't have a full team.

I trudge to the kitchen where Mum is decorating Simon's birthday cake. It's a giant calculator with licorice bits for buttons. Awesome.

I hand Mum the candles. All eight of them.

"Eight is a cool number," says Simon, who's mucking around with cocoa, spoons and scales.

I think for a moment. "A spider has eight legs."

"An octopus has eight tentacles," chimes in Mum.

Simon grins. This is his favourite game. "A tablespoon of cocoa weighs eight grams," he offers.

"Two dogs have eight legs." (That's me again.)

"And four ears," says Dad, who's just walked in and doesn't understand the rules.

Simon takes a deep breath. "There are eight planets in the solar system, and ..." He looks around and spots my soccer jersey, "and ... the Westville Warriors scored eight goals against the Rovers."

I stare at him, surprised. Simon comes to all my soccer games, but I didn't think he actually watched. "Who else did we score eight goals against, Simon?"

He looks up from measuring the circumference of Mum's cooking bowl. "The Falcons."

Jeez.

Even Dad seems impressed. "How many fouls did the Falcons get in that game?" he asks.

"Two," Simon says, jotting down measurements in his notebook. "One for being offside and one for a handball."

Wow! Simon knows heaps about soccer! He sure puts Zola the Bowler to shame.

Suddenly, out of nowhere, a brainwave arrives like a blinding flash. "You're eight today!" I yelp.

Simon doesn't respond. He's moved on to weighing cutlery.

Dad gazes at me as if I've gone bonkers. I don't wait to explain. I rush to my bedroom to grab a copy of the Central District Soccer Rules. Jake's mum sent it around last night.

I rescue the sheet of paper from under my dirty soccer socks. ***Eugh***—the fumes are enough to melt my eyeballs.

I scan the list, and yes!

There it is in black and white.

Simon is old enough to play for the Warriors!

4. Players in the U12 team must be aged 8 and over.

Dad thinks it's a cool idea for Simon to join the team. Anything to avoid a forfeit, he says. Mum isn't so sure. "Simon won't get hurt, will he?"

"He'll only be there to make up the numbers," I tell her. "I'll put him in the midfield, and he can just run up and down. I'll look after him."

Simon insists on carrying the soccer ball across to the sports ground. He traces his finger over the black and white shapes. "There's twelve pentagons and twenty hexagons," he announces.

Funny … I never knew that.

The Warriors swarm around Simon, patting him on the back. "Good on ya, champ."

"Thanks for helping out."

Simon gazes around the soccer pitch with a broad grin. He whips out his tape measure and starts to walk towards the goal box.

"What's he doing?" Oliver Scott asks with a worried look.

"He likes to measure stuff," I explain. "We'll practise around him."

We do some stretches, then I head over to grab the bag of soccer balls. It's empty. I look around. Simon has them lined up along the halfway line.

"***What the***—?"

"Four balls are exactly one metre long," he announces with satisfaction.

The boys start to grumble. "I thought you said Simon was interested in soccer," says Jamil, our goalkeeper.

"Well … he is, sort of."

We decide to practise dribbling around the centre circle, but Simon is there measuring the radius.

"Let's shoot balls into the net," I suggest.

"Wait for me!" yells Simon.

Big phew! Simon is finally going to join in. I grin at him in a friendly way. "You can have first shot, champ."

He looks at me blankly. "No thanks. I want to measure the distance the balls travel."

I try to control my temper. "You can do that later. For now, I want you to join in with us, okay?"

Simon's brow wrinkles, as if he's considering it. He looks towards the goal box and suddenly his face lights up.

"Look at the net," he yells. "Tessellations!"

By the time practice is over, everyone is glad to go home. Everyone except Simon.

"Soccer is a great learning experience," he declares.

It sure is.

CHAPTER 5

FRIDAY: ONE DAY TO GO

"**I'VE GOT A GREAT IDEA**," I tell Rusty.

"Oh man!" he cries, clutching his throat in a totally fake way. "Someone save me from another one of Brad's brainwaves."

Very funny. ***Not.***

Rusty and I are sitting on the bench outside the newspaper office. It's another bright, sunny (rain-free) day in Westville. People walk past casting hopeful looks at the sky.

In case you haven't been counting, it's only one day till the grand final. I've been racking my brain all night to come up with a new plan. Finally I've got one.

"We'll contact the soccer committee and ask for an exemption to the rules. Maybe they'll let us field a team of eight."

"Another brilliant suggestion," says Rusty, "from the Department of Mad Ideas." He takes off his cap and spikes up his hair before turning his grey eyes towards me. "The committee agreed to drop the numbers down to nine, right?"

"Right."

"That's two less than a full team, right?"

"Right again."

He makes his hands into a steeple as if he's thinking deeply. "And it took them two weeks to make that decision, right?"

"Er... yeah." I can see where this is going, and it's not pretty.

He throws his hands wide like a lawyer. "So what are the chances they'll change the rules again twenty-four hours before the grand final?"

I puff out my cheeks. The short answer is ... none. The long answer is zip, zero and zilch.

I pull a crumpled piece of paper out of my pocket. It's the match sheet for tomorrow's game. "We're sunk then. We'll have to enter a forfeit."

Rusty lets out a whine that sounds like a string of vowels. ***"Aaaaeeeeeii."***

I know how he feels. It's not fair. The Tigers will win the trophy without kicking a single ball.

Have I mentioned the Tigers yet? They're from Tumbarilla, a flat, barren place even further west than Westville.

They grow up tough in Tumbarilla, and the Tigers play a mean game of soccer. (And I do mean … er mean.) The captain is Sam and his profile looks something like this.

"I'll leave you to do the evil deed," says Rusty, setting off. "I'll text the rest of the team from Mum's phone."

"Right." I feel my stomach sinking into the footpath. "Let's all meet at noon at the sports ground."

I take out my pen and test it on my shorts. I'm about to scribble ***FORFEIT*** on the match sheet when a voice behind me booms, "Warriors to win!"

It's Mr Wright from the newspaper office. He's at the window sticking up the front page of today's paper.

Mr Wright is a big man and when he grins, his mouth gets swallowed by the rest of his face. He's grinning now and jabbing a stubby finger at the headlines. "Today's lead article should interest a young sportsman like you," he says.

"That sounds exciting," I mumble, as I run my eyes over the headline. "A sporting legend? That's promising!" I continue on to the rest of the article. It's a bit hard to read because the glass is plastered with a year's worth of old sticky tape. But I can make out enough of the article for my heart to start skipping like it's on the Jump Rope team. I can't believe our luck! We could still play in the grand final!

WESTVILLE WEEKLY

THE BEST IN THE WEST

Sporting legend comes to town

By ace reporter Reid Wright

At eleven years old, Casey Croft has earned a reputation as a sporting legend. Basketball, cricket and long-distance running are all fields in which Casey has earned top honours.

The Croft family moved into the old Smith farmhouse on Wednesday…

I don't wait to read any more. Would you? I grab my bike (still two sizes too small) and pedal towards the old farmhouse so fast that air rushes around my ears.

This is like something out of a bad action movie. You know the kind. A bomb is about to blast the city apart and at ten seconds to midnight, the hero (with sweaty brow) *just* manages to cut the wire.

The way I see it, the grand final is the ticking time bomb, and Casey Croft is about to become a hero.

This is one brainwave that won't backfire.

The front verandah of the farmhouse looks like an ad for Sporty's Warehouse. It's strewn with basketballs, cricket gear, a tennis racquet and … I blink and look again … am I seeing things? Nope. Under a tin of tennis balls is a pair of soccer shin guards.

Eureka!

I wipe the sweat from my nose, straighten my sticky T-shirt and tap on the door.

No answer.

I knock a bit harder.

Nothing.

I'm about to hammer with the force of a category one cyclone when the door swings open.

"Yes?"

I'm staring at a small, skinny kid in a pink leotard. A girl. She has choppy, blond hair and the kind of mouth that looks like it's smiling, even when it's not.

"Hi," I blurt. "Can I talk to your brother?"

Instead of racing off, the girl folds her arms and regards me with bright, interested eyes. "What for?"

Jeez. I haven't got time for this. "Uh ... it's about soccer." I peer into the dark hallway, trying to hurry her up. "Is Casey around?"

A smile creeps across her face. "No to the first question and yes to the second," she says.

What? My brain feels like it's stuck inside a tumble dryer. It spins helplessly as I try to make sense of the conversation.

The girl takes pity on me. Or something. "I don't have a brother," she says firmly. "I'm Casey. So who are you and what do you want?"

My jaw drops through the floorboards and heads straight for the centre of the earth. My voice comes out thin and squeaky.

"Um, I'm Brad. It's not important, sorry to bother you. Thanks anyway."

I make a dash for my bike and spin the wheels so fast that dust flies.

As I head for the main road, Casey calls after me, "I've heard about the Warriors' problem. I play soccer by the way."

CHAPTER 6

FRIDAY AFTERNOON: HALF A DAY TO GO

"A GIRL ON THE TEAM?" says Rusty. "No way."

It's noon and we're all sprawled on the sports ground sharing a cosmic-sized packet of chips. Everyone seems to agree that a girl on the team would be a disaster. The conversation swings back and forth.

"Girls aren't as tough as boys."

"She wouldn't be able to keep up."

"We'd have to go easy on her."

"She'd cry like a baby if she got hurt."

Somehow I can't imagine Casey crying like a baby. But I don't say anything. I'm still smarting from my little trip to the farmhouse. Why did I have to run away like a scared chicken?

I take another chip and munch half-heartedly. Normally we'd be stuffing ourselves on pizzas, but with the Angelos gone, Westville is a pizza-free zone.

I guess you could say we're having a kind of farewell. The match sheet is in my pocket, and as soon as we're all here, we're planning to sign all our names to a forfeit.

"I don't want to be around when news gets out," Rusty says. "The whole town will go berserk."

No exaggeration there. My gaze travels around the soccer pitch—the scene of so much sporting glory. Today it looks sad and empty.

A couple of galahs pick seeds out of the grass. A black dog sniffs around the goals.

I'm about to turn back when I see something else. Something that makes my heart leap to my throat.

A skinny kid in baggy shorts has wandered onto the pitch. In her hands is a soccer ball. She balances it on her ankle, kicks it lightly into the air and catches it on her boot. Up and down, up and down. I get dizzy watching.

Next, she dribbles the ball neatly around a couple of make-believe players and pops a shot into the upper corner of the net.

Wow!

I'm on my feet before my brain has time to catch up. Casey sees me coming. She uses her boot to roll the ball towards her, then in one graceful movement kicks it right over my head.

Game on!

I charge down the pitch but Casey beats me to the ball. She drives it forwards at top speed while I try to catch up. Suddenly, she slows right down. This is my big chance. As soon as I'm close, Casey lunges sideways. Left, right, left, right. It's impossible to get anywhere near her.

But Casey hasn't finished. She heads the ball into the air, runs onto it and catches it on her chest. She keeps running towards the goal... and ***thoomp***! It's in.

It takes roughly two seconds to sign Casey up to the Warriors. "You need me, and I need you," she says with a grin. "Next year, I'm going away to a boarding school with a special sports program. Being on the team will help me stay fit."

Everyone's rapt.

"Cool, I've always wanted girls on the team," I hear Jamil declare.

"Me too," says Oliver, as the players wander home.

After everyone's gone, Rusty pulls me aside with a worried look.

"It's a disaster," he says, shaking his head till his gelled spikes quiver.

I nod. "It's a world-class catastrophe."

"Are you thinking what I'm thinking, Einstein?"

"I sure am. With Casey on the team, the rest of us are gunna look ..."

"Pretty average?"

"Totally ordinary."

We grin at one another and slap our hands in a high five.

As I cross the road for home, I should be feeling awesome. But no. A new worry is creeping into my brain.

CHAPTER 7

SATURDAY: THE BIG DAY

WE'RE ON THE FIELD all decked out in our blue and gold. Nick's old jersey fits Casey pretty well. I can hear her breathing beside me. She's run all the way from Crofts' Pizza Parlour. That's right. Casey's mum, Jo Croft, has bought the Angelos' old shop. The team is heading there for pizza after the game.

My eyes flick around the grandstand. Just about everyone in Westville and their dog is here today. The bunch from Tumbarilla makes plenty of noise. Especially when the Tigers trot onto the ground, looking fierce in orange and black.

I don't mind admitting it. I am now entering the panic zone (scary music, please). You see, the Tigers have a reputation for mouthing off. It's a strategy they use during the game to make the opposition lose focus. With a girl on our team, we're an easy target. I can almost hear the smart comments now.

"Ya need a girl to help yez win?"

"What a bunch of losers!"

It could put us right off our game.

My heart thumps so hard in my chest that it competes with a distant roll of thunder. The day is hot. Sticky. A fresh breeze whips up my hair.

The Tigers jog across the grass and line up opposite us. It's a ritual we've pinched from the AFL. I can't bring myself to look into their faces. My eyes burrow into the ground instead.

There's a few hundred minutes of silence. The air grows still and even the birds seem to be holding their breath.

I open my eyes and eyeball the player opposite. I blink and look again. Could it be true? The player is a girl!

Un-bee-lievable!

I tighten my bootlaces, pull up my socks and wait for the toss. Suddenly, I'm ready for anything.

Well, almost ...

WESTVILLE WEEKLY
THE BEST IN THE WEST

Westville celebrates!

By ace reporter Reid Wright

The crowd went wild at the sports ground last Saturday. The Warriors scored an early goal, followed closely by one from the Tigers. It was neck and neck all the way to halftime.

Then the skies opened. Farmers say it's the best rain in seven years. The grand final was a washout and everyone's still cheering!